POEMS
FOR
7
YEAR
OLDS

Also available from
Macmillan Children's Books

Poems for 8 Year Olds
chosen by Matt Goodfellow

The Best Ever Book of Funny Poems
chosen by Brian Moses

Shaping the World: 40 Historical Heroes in Verse
chosen by Liz Brownlee

50 Ways to Score A Goal and other football poems
by Brian Bilston

POEMS FOR 7 YEAR OLDS

A.F. HARROLD

ILLUSTRATED BY ROXANA DE ROND

MACMILLAN CHILDREN'S BOOKS

Published 2022 by Macmillan Children's Books
an imprint of Pan Macmillan
The Smithson, 6 Briset Street, London EC1M 5NR
EU representative: Macmillan Publishers Ireland Ltd, 1st Floor,
The Liffey Trust Centre, 117–126 Sheriff Street Upper
Dublin 1, D01 YC43
Associated companies throughout the world
www.panmacmillan.com

ISBN 978-1-5290-6522-0

The permissions acknowledgements on page 109
constitute an extension of this copyright page.

1 3 5 7 9 8 6 4 2

A CIP catalogue record for this book is available from the British Library.

Printed and bound by CPI Group (UK) Ltd, Croydon CR0 4YY

These pages are made from wood,
mushed and pulped and flattened,
be thankful you weren't up the tree
on the day that that all happened.

When you look closely at this book
you'll find poems on all the pages,
and I hope you like the ones I picked
cos finding them all took me ages.

A. F. Harrold

 # CONTENTS

FORBiDDEN POEM

This poem is not for children.
Keep out!
There is a big oak door
in front of this poem.
It's locked.
And on the door is a notice
in big red letters.
It says: Any child who enters here
will never be the same again.
WARNING. KEEP OUT.

But what's this?
A key in the keyhole.
And what's more,
nobody's about.

'Go on. Look,'
says a little voice
inside your head.
'Surely a poem
cannot strike you dead?'

You turn the key.
The door swings wide.
And then you witness
what's inside.

1

And from that day
you'll try in vain.
You'll never be the same again.

Tony Mitton

THE DRAGON'S CURSE

Enter darkness. Leave the light.
Here be nightmare. Here be fright.
Here be dragon, flame and flight.
Here be spit-fire. Here be grief.
So curse the bones of unbelief.
Curse the creeping treasure-thief.
Curse much worse the dragon-slayer.
Curse his purse and curse his payer.
Curse these words. Preserve their sayer.
Earth and water, fire and air.
Prepare to meet a creature rare.
Enter now, if you dare.
Enter now . . . the dragon's lair!

Nick Toczek

FLiNT

An emerald is as green as grass,
  A ruby red as blood;
A sapphire shines as blue as heaven;
  A flint lies in the mud.

A diamond is a brilliant stone,
  To catch the world's desire;
An opal holds a fiery spark;
  But a flint holds fire.

Christina Rossetti

SPELLS

I dance and dance without any feet —
This is the spell of the ripening wheat.

With never a tongue I've a tale to tell —
This is the meadow-grasses' spell.

I give you health without any fee —
This is the spell of the apple-tree.

I rhyme and riddle without any book —
This is the spell of the bubbling brook.

Without any legs I run for ever —
This is the spell of the mighty river.

I fall for ever and not at all —
This is the spell of the waterfall.

Without a voice I roar aloud —
This is the spell of the thunder-cloud.

No button or seam has my white coat —
This is the spell of the leaping goat.

I can cheat strangers with never a word —
This is the spell of the cuckoo-bird.

We have tongues in plenty but speak no names —
This is the spell of the fiery flames.

The creaking door has a spell to riddle —
I play a tune without any fiddle.

James Reeves

I SAW ESAU

I saw Esau sawing wood,
And Esau saw I saw him;
Though Esau saw I saw him saw,
Still Esau went on sawing.

Anon.

CHOPPING OFF GRANNY'S HEAD

I've gone and chopped off Granny's head
and cut Grandad in half –
I really must learn how to take
a better photograph!

Colin West

I Know an Old Lady

I know an old lady who swallowed a fly.
I don't know why she swallowed a fly –
   perhaps she'll die.

I know an old lady who swallowed a spider,
That wriggled and jiggled and tickled inside her.
She swallowed the spider to catch the fly,
but I don't know why she swallowed the fly –
   perhaps she'll die.

I know an old lady who swallowed a bird.
Now how absurd! to swallow a bird!
She swallowed the bird to catch the spider,
That wriggled and jiggled and tickled inside her.
She swallowed the spider to catch the fly,
but I don't know why she swallowed the fly –
    perhaps she'll die.

I know an old lady who swallowed a cat.
Now fancy that! to swallow a cat!
She swallowed the cat to catch the bird,
She swallowed the bird to catch the spider,
That wriggled and jiggled and tickled inside her.
She swallowed the spider to catch the fly,
but I don't know why she swallowed the fly –
    perhaps she'll die.

I know an old lady who swallowed a dog.
What a hog! to swallow a dog!
She swallowed the dog to catch the cat,
She swallowed the cat to catch the bird,
She swallowed the bird to catch the spider,
That wriggled and jiggled and tickled inside her.
She swallowed the spider to catch the fly,
but I don't know why she swallowed the fly –
    perhaps she'll die.

I know an old lady who swallowed a goat.
She just opened her throat and swallowed a goat!
She swallowed the goat to catch the dog,
She swallowed the dog to catch the cat,
She swallowed the cat to catch the bird,
She swallowed the bird to catch the spider,
That wriggled and jiggled and tickled inside her.
She swallowed the spider to catch the fly,
but I don't know why she swallowed the fly –
    perhaps she'll die.

I know an old lady who swallowed a cow.
I don't know how she swallowed a cow!
She swallowed the cow to catch the goat,
She swallowed the goat to catch the dog,
She swallowed the dog to catch the cat,
She swallowed the cat to catch the bird,
She swallowed the bird to catch the spider,
That wriggled and jiggled and tickled inside her.
She swallowed the spider to catch the fly,
I don't know why she swallowed the fly –
    perhaps she'll die.

I know an old lady who swallowed a horse . . .
She's dead, of course!

                                        Anon.

OUR VISIT TO THE ZOO

When we went to the Zoo
We saw a gnu,
An elk and a whelk
And a wild emu.

We saw a hare
And a bear in his lair,
And a seal have a meal
On a high-backed chair.

We saw a snake
That was hardly awake,
And a lion eat meat
They'd forgotten to bake.

We saw a racoon
And a baby baboon.
The giraffe made us laugh
All afternoon!

We saw a crab
And a long-tailed dab,
 And we all went home
In a taxi-cab.

Jessie Pope

ELEPHANT CLEANERS

The Elephants empty the bins in twos
then wash the floors and clean the loos
they wipe the tops with hairy mops
one works hard whilst the other stops
and yet the truth I must confess
is that they leave the house a mess.

Dom Conlon

DOGS WiTH HUMAN NAMES

Dogs with human names
really make me laugh:
Graham's licking Granny's foot!
Oh, Dave, you need a bath!

Dogs with human names
make me howl so I can't breathe:
Elspeth's had an accident!
Goodness, Peter, please!

Dogs with human names
make me double up and giggle:
Stop it, Mr Stephenson,
you needle when you nibble!

Agatha to Andy
Jennifer to James
I think they're great, let's celebrate
dogs with human names!

Matt Goodfellow

BEE! I'M EXPECTiNG YOU!

Bee! I'm expecting you!
Was saying yesterday
To somebody you know
That you were due.

The frogs got home last week,
Are settled, and at work;
Birds, mostly back,
To clover warm and thick.

You'll get my letter by
the seventeenth; reply
Or better, be with me,
Yours, Fly.

Emily Dickinson

THE TRUTH ABOUT WASPS

The wasp is such a nuisance,
I wouldn't waste your time with it.
Not only might it sting you,
But no other words will rhyme with it.

Mike Barfield

MiGHTY MiDGE
(OR SiZE iSN'T EVERYTHiNG)

I'm a little midge,
a wee black speck,
I like to hover around your neck,
I travel in clouds
but I'm so small,
it's just like I'm not there at all . . .

That's until you feel me nip,
A pesky pinch!
A snarky snip!
Yes, though I'm teeny,
I'm a meanie,
I'll give your arm a tiny peck
And oh good grief it hurts like heck!

Hee hee hee!
Oh, I'm so wee,
No one seems to notice me.

You're the loser!
I'm the winner!
P.S. Thank you for my dinner.

Smriti Halls

HAMMY HAMSTER'S GREAT ADVENTURE

He was sitting on Granny's hand
When he noticed the opening
Between the sleeve of her blouse
And her arm
And decided to investigate

Granny said,
Ooh,
Aah
Eeek
No!
Ouch!
Ooooooooh
Ha!
Hee hee hee
Ah
Ah
No . . . no . . .
Ouch!
Mmmmmmmm
Eek
Ugh!
Aaaaaaaaaaaaaaahhhh . . .
Ah . . .

And Hammy,
Emerging from Granny's left trouser leg,
Said,
Hmmm – that was interesting.
I think I might try it again.

Roger Stevens

HOW DOTH THE
LITTLE CROCODILE

How doth the little crocodile
    Improve his shining tail,
And pour the waters of the Nile
    On every golden scale!

How cheerfully he seems to grin,
    How neatly spreads his claws,
And welcomes little fishes in
    With gently smiling jaws!

Lewis Carroll

MARY HAD A CROCODILE

Mary had a crocodile
That ate a child each day;
But interfering people came
And took her pet away.

Anon.

ELETELEPHONY

Once there was an elephant
Who tried to use the telephant –
No! no! I mean an elephone
Who tried to use the telephone –
(Dear me! I am not certain quite
That even now I've got it right.)
Howe'er it was, he got his trunk
Entangled in the telephunk;
The more he tried to get it free,
The louder buzzed the telephee –
(I fear I'd better drop the song
Of elephop and telephong!)

Laura E. Richards

LEiSURE

What is this life if, full of care,
We have no time to stand and stare?

No time to stand beneath the boughs
And stare as long as sheep or cows.

No time to see, when woods we pass,
Where squirrels hide their nuts in grass.

No time to see, in broad daylight,
Streams full of stars like skies at night.

No time to turn at Beauty's glance,
And watch her feet, how they can dance.

No time to wait till her mouth can
Enrich that smile her eyes began.

A poor life this if, full of care,
We have no time to stand and stare.

W. H. Davies

GO EXPLORE THE COUNTRYSIDE

A summer's day, a bunch of friends
Bows and arrows, building dens
Make believe and let's pretend
All of this and much more when
Finding tallest trees to climb
Leave reality behind
Hide and seek and lots to find
Losing track of space and time
A place to chase and seek and hide
Go explore the countryside

Rope swings over muddy ditches
Stepping stones and building bridges
Snagging clothes on hawthorn hedges
Balancing on stony ledges
Buttercups beneath the chin
Spinning jennies spin and spin
Grass between the thumbs that sing
Dock leaf cures for nettle stings
Hikes to hike and bikes to ride
Go explore the countryside

A piece of penknife poetry
Initialled love hearts there to see
Carved graffiti on the tree
From here to eternity
Flat and smooth skimming stones
Four-leaf clovers, pine cones
Branches look like monster bones
Escape from all the mobile phones
All of these and more beside
Go explore the countryside

Be a cowboy, be a pirate
Let the geography inspire it
Be a soldier, be a knight
Find that stick to fight that fight
Forest shadows, grass that's high
A place to laugh or shout or cry
Caves and bones and stones and rocks
Blowing dandelion clocks
Imagination – far and wide
Go explore the countryside

Let your dog run and run
Lose your dad and hide from Mum
There is space for everyone
In God's fairground filled with fun
Time for families to run wild
Find that hidden inner child

A fallen tree's a crocodile
Lose yourself and stay awhile
Feel the secrets on the breeze
Feel the past within the trees
Eternity in flowing streams
Rugged rocks and crystal streams

Go explore, go explore
Go explore – it's what it's for
All of this and much, much more
Mother Nature's superstore
Where geography, biology
And history all collide
There's majesty and mystery
Passing time for me and you
Lots of things to make and do
Yesterdays or something new
Go explore – you know it's true

The magic here, the magic there
Take your time to stop and stare
Be sanctified and goggle-eyed
Satisfied and gratified
Come back to
Come back to
The magic of the countryside

Paul Cookson

THE SUN QUEEN

Afternoon

She   Sun.

Sun   My queen.

She   Where have you gone?

Sun   Behind the cloud.

She   Won't you come out?

Sun   I'm afraid I can't.

She   Is there nothing to do?

Sun   You could call the wind to move the cloud.

She   OK. Where is the wind?

Sun   Behind the rain.

She   Where is the rain?

Sun   Hidden in the cloud.

She   Which one?

Sun   I don't know. I can't see from here.

She   You play too many games.

Zaro Weil

WHEN FISHES SET UMBRELLAS UP

When fishes set umbrellas up
  If the rain-drops run,
Lizards will want their parasols
  To shade them from the sun.

Christina Rossetti

THE TROLL SPEAKS OUT

That's not how it happened!
Now I've had enough –
I'm dishing the dirt
On the Billy Goats Gruff.

There was no 'Fol-de-Rol',
No field of green grass,
No rickety bridge –
The whole thing's a farce.

I was tending my roses,
(I'd mended the bridge),
When I saw the three goats
Coming over the ridge.

I went forward to meet them,
My arms open wide.
'I've got some Swiss roll –
Won't you all come inside?'

One suddenly charged;
It was like a bad dream.
I flew through the air,
Landing 'Splosh!' in the stream.

By the time I crawled out,
All covered in gunk,
They'd eaten my roses
And then done a bunk.

And that's the plain truth –
It's the worst of all scandals!
Those Billy Goats Gruff
Are nothing but vandals.

Hilda Offen

ADVICE TO RAPUNZEL

Sort yourself out.
   Don't hang around
   for someone else to rescue you.

Give yourself a trim.
   Pick up the scissors,
   it's not rocket science.

Make a rope ladder.
   Twist one. Plait one. Improvise.
   Use your head for more than growing hair.

Escape.
   Secure the ladder.
   Shimmy down and leg it.

Don't look back.
   Get clean away.
   Vamoose. Stay loose.

And learn your lesson.
   Staying put beneath a tyrant's thumb
   is dumb.

Jan Dean

WANTED: WIZARD'S ASSISTANT

QUALIFICATIONS
Candidate must be:

proficient at palm puzzling
scroll scribbling
and potent potion pondering
spiffing at spell spotting
good at goblin gobbling
a champion at chanting
and wonderful with wobsicles

JOB DESCRIPTION
Includes, but not limited to:

magic marshmallow making on Mondays
tea leaf translating on Tuesdays
wand wobbling on Wednesdays
thunder formation on Thursdays
frightening frogs on Fridays

DEADLINE FOR APPLICATIONS
Yesterday

Laura Mucha

THE SPY CAFÉ

The Spy Café's a peculiar place.

The sign on the door only ever says CLOSED.

They keep the lighting way down low
and the menu's written in invisible ink.

The special of the day is usually Spy Pie
(with the filling kept TOP SECRET).

No one has *ever seen the cook.*

The spies don't say much,
preferring to ink coded messages on napkins
and leave them casually on the other spies' plates.

The waiters wear wigs and dark glasses.

They mutter things like

   the badger is in the hole

to nobody in particular.

I'd suggest we meet for a cup of tea
but the Spy Café can be difficult to find.

Very difficult to find.

Very, very difficult to find.

Kate Wakeling

LOCH NESS WARNING

When the loch is big
and the loch is deep
and the sides slope down
like cliffside steep
and you can't see the bottom
and it's cold as night
don't go swimming
or you'll end up a bite
of a human nugget
in the monster's belly
and you'll rot beside fish
and a fisherman's welly
that he lost in the loch
when he ran from the sight
of the serpenty head
poking into the light
on the day that he caught
his hook on a whopper
and the monster roared
and he thought he'd come a cropper
but to his surprise
his legs went round
and he zipped up the beach
and all Nessie found
was one lost boot

and a couple of fish
which she gobbled straight up,
then vanished with a splish
and a gurgle as she sank
back beneath the water
waiting for a swimmer
who really shouldn't oughta
swim in the loch
so cold and so deep
where a hungry monster's
always ready to eat.

A. F. Harrold

THE MAD GARDENER'S SONG

He thought he saw an Elephant,
  That practised on a fife:
He looked again, and found it was
  A letter from his wife.
'At length I realize,' he said,
  'The bitterness of Life!'

He thought he saw a Buffalo
  Upon the chimney-piece:
He looked again, and found it was
  His Sister's Husband's Niece.
'Unless you leave this house,' he said,
  'I'll send for the police!'

He thought he saw a Rattlesnake
  That questioned him in Greek:
He looked again, and found it was
  The Middle of Next Week.
'The one thing I regret,' he said,
  'Is that it cannot speak!'

He thought he saw a Banker's Clerk
  Descending from the bus:
He looked again, and found it was
  A Hippopotamus:
'If this should stay to dine,' he said,
  'There won't be much for us!'

He thought he saw a Kangaroo
  That worked a coffee-mill:
He looked again, and found it was
  A Vegetable-Pill.
'Were I to swallow this,' he said,
  'I should be very ill!'

He thought he saw a Coach-and-Four
  That stood beside his bed:
He looked again, and found it was
  A Bear without a Head.
'Poor thing,' he said, 'poor silly thing!
  It's waiting to be fed!'

He thought he saw an Argument
  That proved he was the Pope:
He looked again, and found it was
  A Bar of Mottled Soap.
'A fact so dread,' he faintly said,
  'Extinguishes all hope!'

Lewis Carroll

WiSHES OF AN ELDERLY MAN

I wish I loved the Human Race;
I wish I loved its silly face;
I wish I liked the way it walks;
I wish I liked the way it talks;
And when I'm introduced to one
I wish I thought *What Jolly Fun!*

Sir Walter A. Raleigh

THE RASH LADY OF RYDE

There was an old lady of Ryde
Who ate some green apples, and died.
The apples (fermented inside the lamented)
Made cider inside 'er inside.

Anon.

APPRECiATION

Auntie, did you feel no pain
Falling from that willow tree?
Will you do it, please, again?
Cos my friend here didn't see.

Harry Graham

GRANDPAPA

Grandpapa fell down a drain;
Couldn't scramble out again.
Now he's floating down the sewer,
There's one grandpapa the fewer.

Harry Graham

INFANT INNOCENCE

The grizzly bear is huge and wild;
He has devoured the infant child.
The infant child is not aware
He has been eaten by the bear.

A. E. Housman

TO THE MOON

O Moon! when I look on your beautiful face
Careering along through the darkness of space,
The thought has quite frequently come to my mind
If ever I'll gaze on your lovely behind.

Anon.

WELCOME TO THE BOOKSHOP

Hello, explorer.
Hello, time traveller.
Hello, wordsmith and translator.

Hello, learner and watcher.
Hello, listener and grower.

Hello, librocubicularist.
(That's those who like to read in bed.)

Here's a map.   Mind the gap.

On the first floor, there be dragons.
On the second, flying lessons.
On the third floor there's a forest.
On the fourth, a choir of sonnets.
On the fifth, if you're quick,
you can discuss politics
with any character from history.
On the sixth, let's solve a mystery.
When you're done, pull up a seat,
we'll have some cake and drink some tea.

Check for crumbs, crack that spine,
choose which words to underline.

Hello, you.
Hello, reader.

Welcome home.

Jen Campbell

A POEM TO BE SPOKEN SiLENTLY . . .

It was so silent that I heard
my thoughts rustle
like leaves in a paper bag . . .

It was so peaceful that I heard
the trees ease off
their coats of bark . . .

It was so still that I heard
the paving stones groan
as they muscled for space . . .

It was so silent that I heard
a page of this book
whisper to its neighbour,
'Look, he's peering at us again . . .'

It was so still that I felt
a raindrop grin
as it tickled the window's pane . . .

It was so calm that I sensed
a smile crack
the wary face
of a stranger . . .

It was so quiet that I heard
the morning earth roll over
in its sleep and doze
for five minutes more . . .

Pie Corbett

WORDS

There are words
and there are
words
and there are words that send you

                                  t
                                   u
                                    m
                                      b
                                        l
                                          i
                                            n
                                                g

and words that gather-you-up

and words that   push you
                                      away

                   and words that
pull you back
and words that sing about love and home and feel
   like a warm glug of soup on a grey day, like sodden
   socks drying by the hearth.
And there are words
that are final.
That stop
you mid

walk. That fold you in half and bury you in the
     ground so fast thatyouhardlyhavetimetobreathe.
All these words, these small words,
they hold such power,
such greatness,
they are mighty, so mighty, when they are work
     together, woven in lines, stitching
corners of a poem tight, stronger than rope,
but those words, those small, small words are
     somehow mighty even when they are

alone.

They hang

                              free

wherever they please
unbound
                    unfettered.

Clever little things,
those
words.

Swapna Haddow

PURE POETRY

A chicken's cluck
and the quack of a duck,
the moo of a cow
and the oink of a sow,
a donkey's bray
and the words we say –
that's pure poetry.

A pea pod's pop
and a chopstick's chop,
an alphabetti mumble
and a big belly rumble,
a bubble's squeak
and the words we speak –
that's pure poetry.

A greedy slurp
and a burst of burps,
a whistling wheeze
and a sploshy sneeze,
swish 'em all about
with the words we shout –
that's pure poetry.

A muttering mother
and a big-mouthed brother,
an auntie ranting
and a puppy panting,
a giggling sister
and the words we whisper —
that's pure poetry.

A canteen's clatter
and a classroom's chatter,
a seagull's screech
and the waves on a beach,
the swish of a swing
and the words we sing —
that's pure poetry.

Steve Tasane

I Like Eating in the Bath

Eating in the bath
Eating in the bath
I like eating in the bath.

I like eating strawberry jelly in the bath
I like eating marmalade in the bath
I like eating chocolate in the bath
I like eating peach yogurt in the bath.

Eating in the bath
Eating in the bath
I like eating in the bath.

I like eating Victoria sponge cake in the bath
I like eating knickerbocker glories in the bath
I like eating vanilla ice cream with a flake in the bath
I like eating apple crumble and custard in the bath.

Eating in the bath
Eating in the bath
I like eating in the bath.

I like eating scrambled eggs in the bath
I like eating toast and baked beans in the bath
I like eating fish fingers in the bath
I like eating pepperoni pizza in the bath.

Eating in the bath
Eating in the bath
I like eating in the bath.

I like eating sausage and mash in the bath
I like eating peanut butter in the bath
I like eating chicken nuggets in the bath
I like eating hamburgers in the bath.

Eating in the bath
Eating in the bath
I like eating in the bath.

I like eating pancakes in the bath
I like eating fish and chips in the bath
I like eating spaghetti bolognese in the bath
I like eating roast potatoes, juicy succulent chicken,
    golden Yorkshire pudding
and lots and lots of lovely gravy in the bath.

Eating in the bath
Eating in the bath
I like eating in the bath.

Kat François

Disappointing Lemonade

There's nothing quite as nice
As lemonade with ice.
Unless it's gone unbubbly,
Which isn't half as lubbly.

Jo Cotterill

MANNERS

I eat my peas with honey,
I've done it all my life.
It makes them taste quite funny,
But it keeps them on the knife.

Anon.

'WARE TOMATO JUICE

An accident happened to my brother Jim
When somebody threw a tomato at him –
Tomatoes are juicy and don't hurt the skin,
But this one was specially packed in a tin.

Anon.

EAT YOUR VEG

Go on, try the artichoke,
Yes I agree they look
A bit unappetising,
But that TV cook

That you like, gave us the recipe,
And it doesn't taste too bad,
Well how about the peas then?
They're the best *I've* ever had.

What do you mean onions and peppers,
Are too crunchy when you chew?
That's the lamest excuse ever,
Just try a piece . . . won't you?

These tomatoes are full of vitamins,
Oh yes, you hate the seeds,
Will you taste the aubergine?
Then how about some swedes?

Daddy's done these parsnips specially,
Would you like a wedge?
Oh, come on, don't be difficult,
Mummy, eat your veg.

Valerie Bloom

Be Nice to the Rhubarb

The fruit shop is busy.
Apples talking, pears walking.
The plum placates as the banana cries.
In the corner there, grapes gang up
On the lonely rhubarb.
'Be nice to the rhubarb,' says Miss Dorothy.
'If you don't behave, I'm making a smoothie.'

Chitra Soundar

THE GOOD AND THE CLEVER

If all the good people were clever,
And all clever people were good,
The world would be nicer than ever
We thought that it possibly could.

But somehow, 'tis seldom or never
The two hit it off as they should;
The good are so harsh to the clever,
The clever so rude to the good!

So friends, let it be our endeavour
To make each by each understood;
For few can be good, like the clever,
Or clever so well as the good.

Elizabeth Wordsworth

DEAR SUITCASE

Your lock doesn't work,
your handle is so short,
filled with toys and books
you're so heavy my arms snap in two!
I wish you had a zip.
And a bit of a secret pocket
where I could slip in all that stuff I don't want anyone
   to see –
like the shiniest coin ever I found in the park,
stuck in the oak tree bark
and I'm sure somebody's still looking for it
so I keep it somewhere shhhh.
And obviously my diary,
little stripy pad of paper I stapled together myself.
Fill it up with feelings, thoughts and really funny things.
Sad things too, if I have to. Which I do.
But suitcase, you have no zip
and you have no wheels.
Which feels very unfair cos so many suitcases have
   wheels these days.
I suppose it is good if the road is rocky
or the path is muddy and sodden.
I guess it's true you can carry clothes and pens and paper
   and games –

so maybe you're not so bad after all.
I thought this was a letter of complaint but . . .
I'd just like to stop using you so much, to be honest.
I'm going to ask my mum if we can just stay this time.
I hope that's okay and you find something else to do
     with your days.

Thanks,

Sabrina Mahfouz

IN THE COFFEE SHOP

Why does Mam drink coffee?
It always makes her sad
She stirs her coffee round and round
While she thinks of Dad

She told me they would meet here
Long before I came
Now Dad is living somewhere else
And Mam is not the same

'Mam,' I say, 'Don't worry
We will be okay
You and me together
I won't go away.'

She doesn't even hear me
Mam is in a dream
She takes the spoon and eats the froth
Like it is ice cream

Then she drinks the coffee
But it makes her sigh
Like she doesn't want it
So I wonder why

Why does Mam drink coffee
When it makes her sad?
It costs a lot of money
And it never brings back Dad

Cat Weatherill

THREE SAMPLER VERSES*

By 'Tabitha Anon'

Sweet it is to be a child
Tender merciful and mild
Ever ready to perform
Acts of kindness to a worm.

---

* *In the olden days, before they invented the television, to keep little girls busy and to prepare them for the boredom of being a grown-up, they did sewing and embroidery practically all the time. To display their skills they would embroider little pictures and scenes and Bible verses and personal poems on a single piece of linen, and this 'example' piece is what's called a 'sampler'. Some of these got framed and hung up (like parents today might stick a child's drawing up on the fridge with a magnet) and you can still find them, sometimes, in old antique shops. Sometimes these samplers, from a hundred or two hundred years ago are the only record we have that this person ever lived.*

By Sarah Pelham, 'in the sixth year of her age'

When i was Young
and in my Prime
here you may see
how I spent my time:

By 'Ann Bell'

This is my Work so
You may see. what
care my mother as
took of me. ann bell.

WHAT I REALLY MEAN

(A FOUND POEM)

I didn't say she stole my money.
(But someone said she did.)

I **didn't** say she stole my money.
(I really, really didn't.)

I didn't **say** she stole my money.
(Perhaps I gave a hint.)

I didn't say **she** stole my money.
(But someone must have done it.)

I didn't say she **stole** my money.
(I think she may have hidden it.)

I didn't say she stole **my** money.
(But she did take someone else's.)

I didn't say she stole my **money**.
(I said she stole my glasses.)

Rachel Rooney

MAX IS NOT IN SCHOOL

Today the sun shines
a little bit brighter.
Today the wind has lost
its bite, and the air
hangs less heavy
in the classroom.

Today Max
is not in school.

Today my ears are not stung
by barbed words.
Today my ribs don't tighten
in my chest
as taunts lash out
across the playground.

Today my books
are in my bag
and not torn up and scattered
across the floor.
There's a small oasis
in the wide parched desert;
a faint rainbow
in the winter storm.

Today I can breathe
just for a while

because Max
is not in school.

Joshua Seigal

LOST SMiLE

Sometimes I just can't.
Not even by attaching the corners
of my mouth to my ear lobes
with bright yellow pegs.

Not even by hanging upside down
and allowing gravity to smile for me.
These stubborn cheeks still escape
looking happy.

I've tried forcing a smile and then
lodging my head in the freezer,
but all that freeze are my eyebrows,
like two frozen slugs.

My smile has gone away,
but I don't know where,
each day I wake up,
and still, it isn't there.

I just hope that it finds me,
so I can lose this disguise,
as pretend smiles don't hide
the sadness in my eyes.

Alex Wharton

INSIDE ME

I hid something inside me.

The deeper it hid, the louder it got.
The longer it hid, the sharper it got.

The louder and sharper it got,
It made my inside dark.

Can I crack it open and share it with you?
If you listen, you might let some light through.

Chitra Soundar

LOVE

I will be the friend who will always see you right,
tell you I love you, even when you're being a twit.

I will hold your heart when it's been ripped out.
I whisper to you to help the days move along.

I will leave kisses on your pillow.
I will wipe the blood from your hands
when you have fallen hard.

Sometimes I'm a fool and I don't help
you like I should.
Sometimes I'm just not enough.

Sometimes you just don't understand
love's a two-way thing,
I try to take up any slack.

Like a bud becomes blossom, becomes seed.
Like a midnight feast, a rustling duvet, a solid fact.
I keep on trying for you, to give you what you need.

John Siddique

Old Brown Bear

Old brown bear was an adventurer.
He climbed mountains, crossed rivers,
Catching fish with his bare paws.
His muscles rippled at the slightest threat:
He once fought a mountain lion,
Tore it like tissue paper, and ate his fill.

But now he just sits at the bottom of my bed,
Next to Paddington, who has also seen better times.
They both prefer the days gone by,
When they were at the mercy of my narration,
When they were released into the wild
Imaginings of a boy with stories to tell.

Coral Rumble

AUTUMN SPEAKS TO THE LEAVES

'Won't you *please*
get off the trees!?'

A. F. Harrold

EYE CAN SEE YOU

The conker in its prickly shell
Looked like an eye
On the ground where it fell.
A big brown eye
With a spikey green lid.
And it winked at me.
I'm sure it did.

Mike Barfield

How To Turn Into A Cat

Arch your back,

Stick out your claws,

Disappear for a year then walk back into the kitchen
as if it was yesterday.

Purr at other cats on the television,

Slide your tail along your owner's leg,

Flip the cat flap over and over,

Spin the toilet roll on its holder,

Chase your tail for so long that your owner gets dizzy
watching you.

Jump at your reflection in the oven door,

Stretch out so magnificently on the living room floor
that no one can get by,

Wait quietly on the fence for birds to fly to the
birdfeeder,

Dive head first into a cardboard box,

Dive out of a cardboard box and scare the dog,

Hide under the duvet until someone finds you and then SCREETCH!

Chrissie Gittins

Some 'Counting Out' Rhymes for the Playground

From Walter de la Mare's childhood

Eena, deena, deina, duss,
Catala, weena, weina, wuss,
Spit, spot, must be done,
Twiddlum, twaddlum, twenty-one!

A long one

Hinty, minty, cuty, corn,
Apple seed, and apple thorn,
Wire, briar, limber lock,
Three geese in a flock.
One flew east, and one flew west,
One flew over the cuckoo's nest.
  Up on yonder hill.
That is where my father dwells;
He has jewels, he has rings,
He has many pretty things.
He has a hammer with two nails,
He has a cat with twenty tails.
Strike Jack, lick Tom!
  Blow the bellows, old man!

A Cornish example

Ena, mena, bora mi;
Kisca, lara, mora di;
Eggs, butter, cheese, bread;
Stick, stock, stone dead.

Duck-and-Drake

A Duck and a Drake,
And a ha'penny cake,
And a penny to pay the old baker;
A hop and a scotch is another notch,
Slitherum, slatherum, take her!

Anon.

TWO OR THREE CHRISTMAS SONGS FROM THE PLAYGROUND

To the tune of . . .

Jingle bells, Batman smells,
Robin ran away.
Wonder Woman lost her bra
on the M1 motorway. Hey!

To the tune of . . .

We three kings
of Orient are.
One in a taxi,
one in a car.
One on a scooter beeping his hooter
following yonder star.

Anon.

Now here's a space for you to write down what you sing in your playground when you swap about the words to a well-known tune . . .

I'VE GOT A STiCKER
(BUT I DON'T KNOW WHY)

Today I got a sticker
I got it in my school
it's nice and new and shiny
I think it's really cool
but ask me why I got it
and my thoughts run dry
I've got a sticker
    but I don't know why

It could be cos I painted
a picture of a lake
it could be for baking
a chewy, chocky cake
it could be cos I made a kite
and flew it really high
I've got a sticker
    but I don't know why

I've got this little sticker
it's got a smiley face
I stuck it on my jumper
cos it's my favourite place
maybe I got it
cos I made an apple pie
I've got a sticker
    but I don't know why

It could be cos I'm friendly
Helping people out
It could be cos my teacher
Never has to shout
It could be cos I work hard
And really, really try
I've got a sticker
    But I don't know why

If nobody tells me
I think I'm gonna cry
Cos I've got a sticker
and I don't know why

Craig Bradley

WHEN MS SMITH SLAMMED THE CLASSROOM DOOR

It frightened a flock of pigeons on the back field.
It made the Yorkshire puddings
collapse with a sigh.

It didn't crack ceilings.
It didn't make wars.
It didn't make the summer holidays any shorter.

But it did play on our minds
over and over again.

Mandy Coe

JOHNNY ONE-ARM

So I said to my buddy Rich one day,
'I wonder what it's like to have
just the one arm . . .'

'How should I know!' said Rich, spitting
another peanut shell across the yard.
'Don't ask me, pal. Ask Johnny One-Arm.'

'Johnny One-Arm?' I said. 'No way!'
'Why not?' asked Rich. 'Well,' I said,
'because he's only got one arm.'

'Don't be so soft,' said Rich and he
marched us both across the yard to where
Johnny One-Arm was standing and said,

'Hey, Johnny One-Arm. Dave here
wants to know what it's like.'
'What what's like?' said Johnny One-Arm,

while I turned scarlet from snout to tail.
'*You know*,' said Rich, nodding towards
the space where a left arm would ordinarily be.

Johnny One-Arm thought about it
for a bit then shrugged and said,
'It's okay I guess. Sort of normal.

'Good in some ways. Like I can duck out
of boring cricket practice. Bad in others – wish
I was right-handed. But mostly

just normal,' and then somehow we
got on to other topics and found out
that Johnny One-Arm's into music and bikes

and comic books just like us and since then,
me and Rich and Johnny hang out all the time
and play music and ride bikes and argue

about who's the best comic book hero ever.
One time, Johnny kept saying that Iron Man's
about as interesting as ink drying

and I blew my top, called him
a dumb one-armed freak . . .

so he called me a dumb freckle-faced freak
and then Rich jumped in and called us both
a pair of dumb skinny-legged freaks

then we all pretended to sulk for a while
but soon got bored of that and went for burgers
and ice cream like we always do on Fridays.

Me, Rich and Johnny.
The Five Arms Brothers.

Shauna Darling Robertson

POEM WRiTTEN AFTER UPSETTiNG A WiTCH AT THE WATERiNG HOLE

I go to school every day.
I am not huge and great and grey.

My teeth are short and don't poke out
of my mouth when I pout.

My ears are there at the side
but will not flap in shame or pride.

On my head, at the front,
is a nose and not a trunk.

I've a hunch, I'm fairly sure,
I'm not an elephant any more.

A. F. Harrold

GET A WRIGGLE ON

Get a wriggle on
when you're late for school,
when the car's stuck in traffic
and Mum's lost her cool.

Get a wriggle on
if you're running late,
if the clock's beaten you,
don't sit here and wait.

Get a wriggle on,
quick get out the door,
you're slow as a snail
don't delay any more.

Get a wriggle on
when the sky turns black
when you're caught in the rain
and the thunder cracks.

Get a wriggle on
when the day's getting dark,
but you've lost little brother
and they're closing the park.

Get a wriggle on,
you'll be late for your tea,
get a wriggle on
but wait . . .

Wait for meeeeeeee.

Brian Moses

SECRET PATH

When I was your age,
Grandad told me,
There was a secret path

It ran along the edge
Of the allotments
Down the snake's back
Through the hawthorn trees
To the brickfields
And the dragon's lair

And there,
Grandad said,
We hid from the elves and trolls
And hatched plans
And ate our cheese and pickle sandwiches

Now the secret path
Is a housing estate
But the names of the roads
Remind everyone

Hawthorn Avenue
Snake Alley
Brick Lane
Elves Court
Dragon's Close

Roger Stevens

THE LEGEND OF NEVERMORE LANE

Nobody walks
down Nevermore Lane
in case they're never seen again
lost in the mist
the wind and rain
a mystery, hard to explain

A lane of shadows
of secrets of old
of horror stories seldom told
of whispered warnings
to behold
of screams to make your blood run cold

So walk the lane now
if you dare
go on tiptoe but beware
your eyes play tricks
somehow, somewhere
you'll see things that are not there

By lightning strike
by thunder crack
your footsteps echo down the track
you've gone too far
turn back, turn back
you're face to face with the woman in black

So heed my warning
everyone
one minute you're there
the next you're gone
and the legend of the lane

                    lives on . . .

                    Craig Bradley

I Like To Stay Up

I like to stay up
and listen
when big people talking
jumbie stories

I does feel
so tingly and excited
inside me

But when my mother say
'Girl, time for bed'

Then is when
I does feel a dread

Then is when
I does jump into me bed

Then is when
I does cover up
from me feet to me head

Then is when
I does wish I didn't listen
to no stupid jumbie story

Then is when
I does wish I did read
me book instead.

Grace Nichols

NIGHT SONG

I sing of night, of hunting cats and stars,
Night-dark fences, rimed birch branches,
Black-topped roads, headlamps, cars.

I sing of night, of campfires and owls,
Silkspun spider traps, dripping water taps,
Moonlit mushroom caps, hound howls.

I sing of night, or hoarfrost and dreams,
Goblin haunts and graveyard stones,
What is, and is not what it seems.

Steven Withrow

NiGHT JOURNEY

When it's like this,

when Mum is driving
and everyone is quiet,
heads toppling with sleep,
and the motorway is dizzy black,
slicked with lights,

when it's like this,
the car is not a mile machine.

It is a thought machine.

New thoughts fizz from nowhere.

New thoughts tick and gleam,
find strange shapes,
strange colours,
build things,
grow wings.

New thoughts sizzle out into the dark.

Old thoughts find new homes,
new roads
or
pop like bubbles.

Worries go slow mo,
fade to grey
and vanish.

Because the car is not a mile machine.

It is a thought machine.

Kate Wakeling

WAKiNG UP

Oh! I have just had such a lovely dream!
And then I woke.
And all the dream went out like kettle-steam,
Or chimney-smoke.

My dream was all about – how funny though!
I've only just
Dreamed it, and now it has begun to blow
Away like dust.

In it went – no! in my dream I had –
No, that's not it!
I can't remember, oh, it is *too* bad,
My dream a bit.

But I saw something beautiful, I'm sure –
Then someone spoke,
And then I didn't see it any more,
Because I woke.

Eleanor Farjeon

ABOUT THE AUTHOR

A. F. Harrold is an English poet (1975–present) who writes and performs for adults and children. He is the owner of many books, a handful of hats, a few good ideas and one beard. He spends his time showing off on stage, writing poems and books, and stroking his beard (it helps churn the ideas). He lives in Reading with his partner, Iszi Lawrence (another children's author, go check out her books), and their two cats, Vincent and Susan.

www.afharroldkids.com

ABOUT THE ILLUSTRATOR

Roxana de Rond is a freelance illustrator with a passion for drawing people and dogs. After years of moving between the States and the UK, she settled in Cambridge. In 2016 Roxana graduated with an MA in Children's Book Illustration at Anglia Ruskin University. Her book *Monty and Mortimer* was highly commended for the Macmillan prize and is now being published with Child's Play under the new name *Monty and Milo*.

ACKNOWLEDGEMENTS

The compiler and publisher would like to thank the following for permission to use their copyright material:

Barfield, Mike: 'Eye Can See You' and 'The Truth About Wasps' by Mike Barfield. Copyright © Mike Barfield 2022. Used by kind permission of the poet. **Bloom, Valerie:** 'Eat Your Veg' from *Hot Like Fire* (Bloomsbury, 2000) by Valerie Bloom. Copyright © Valerie Bloom. Used by kind permission of Eddison Pearson on behalf of Valerie Bloom. **Bradley, Craig:** 'I've Got a Sticker (But I Don't Know Why)' and 'The Legend of Nevermore Lane' by Craig Bradley. Copyright © Craig Bradley 2022. Used by kind permission of the poet. **Campbell, Jen:** 'Welcome to the Bookshop' by Jen Campbell. Copyright © Jen Campbell 2022. Used by kind permission of the poet. www.jen-campbell.co.uk. **Coe, Mandy:** 'When Ms Smith Slammed the Classroom Door' from *If you Could See Laughter* (Salt Publishing, 2010) by Mandy Coe. Copyright © Mandy Coe. Used by kind permission of the poet. **Conlon, Dom:** 'Elephant Cleaners' by Dom Conlon. Copyright © Dom Conlon 2022. Used by kind permission of the poet. **Cookson, Paul:** 'Go Explore the Countryside' from *The Very Best of Paul Cookson: Let No One Steal Your Dreams and Other Poems* (Macmillan, 2018) by Paul Cookson. Copyright © Paul Cookson. Used by kind permission of the poet. **Corbett, Pie:** 'A Poem to be Spoken Silently...' from *Evidence of Dragons* (Macmillan, 2011) by Pie Corbett. Copyright © Pie Corbett. Used by kind permission of the poet. **Cotterill, Jo:** 'Disappointing Lemonade' by Jo Cotterill. Copyright © Jo Cotterill 2022. Used by kind permission of the poet. **Dean, Jan:** 'Advice to Rapunzel' from *Reaching the Stars* (Macmillan, 2017) by Jan Dean. Copyright © Jan Dean. Used by kind permission of the poet. **Farjeon, Eleanor:** 'Waking Up' from *Blackbird has Spoken* (Macmillan) by Eleanor Farjeon. Copyright © Eleanor Farjeon. Used by kind permission of David Higham Associates. **François, Kat:** 'I Like Eating in the Bath' by Kat François first published in *Midnight Feasts* (Bloomsbury, 2019). Copyright © Kat François 2019. Used by kind permission of the poet. **Gittins, Chrissie:** 'How to Turn into a Cat' by Chrissie Gittins. Copyright © Chrissie Gittins 2022. Used by kind permission of the poet. **Goodfellow, Matt:** 'Dogs with Human Names' from *Bright Bursts of Colour* (Bloomsbury, 2020) by Matt Goodfellow. Copyright © Matt Goodfellow. Used by kind permission of the poet. **Haddow, Swapna:** 'Words' by Swapna Haddow. Copyright © Swapna Haddow 2022. Used by kind permission of the poet c/o Caroline Sheldon Literary Agency Ltd. **Halls, Smriti:** 'Mighty Midge (Or Size Isn't Everything)' by Smriti Halls. Copyright © Smriti Halls 2022. Used by kind permission of the poet. **Harrold, A. F.:** 'Autumn Speaks to the Leaves', 'Poem Written After Upsetting a Witch at a Watering Hole', 'Loch Ness Warning' and the Dedication

Weatherill, Cat: 'In the Coffee Shop' by Cat Weatherill. Copyright © Cat Weatherill 2022. Used by kind permission of the poet. **Weil, Zaro:** 'The Sun Queen' from *Firecrackers* (Zazakids Books, in association with Troika Books, 2018) by Zaro Weil. Copyright © Zaro Weil. Used by kind permission of the poet. **West, Colin:** 'Chopping Off Granny's Head' by Colin West. Copyright © Colin West. Used by kind permission of the poet. **Wharton, Alex:** 'Lost Smile' from *Daydreams and Jellybeans* (Firefly Press Ltd, 2021) by Alex Wharton. Copyright © Alex Wharton. Used by kind permission of the poet. **Withrow, Steven:** 'Night Song' by Steven Withrow. Copyright © Steven Withrow 2022. Used by kind permission of the poet. **All the anonymous poets of the past:** thank you for leaving your poems hanging around in the world for us to remember and learn and share. **Lewis Carroll, W. H. Davies, Emily Dickinson, Harry Graham, A.E. Housman, Jessie Pope, Sir Walter A. Raleigh** (not the one with the boat)**, Laura E. Richards, Christina Rossetti** and **Elizabeth Wordsworth:** you're no longer around for us to need to pay you for your poems, but I wanted to say thank you for putting such wonderful work (beautiful, funny, moving, daft) out into the world, and to let your shades know, wherever they are right now, that we remember your words and share them because this is what poetry does: speak from one generation to the next, pass those messages along, mouth to mouth from the past to the future. Thank you all. – AFH, 2022